FOR GAMERS EVERYWHERE.
—MW

FOR MY FAMILY, ESPECIALLY CARLOS AND MY DOGS.
AND FOR THOSE WHO ARE HERE,
AND THOSE WHO ARE NO LONGER WITH US.
—BC

union
square
kids

NEW YORK

Text © 2020 Marcie Wessels
Cover and Interior Illustrations © 2020 Beatriz Castro

ISBN 978-1-4549-3259-8

For information about custom editions, special sales, and premium purchases,
please contact specialsales@unionsquareandco.com.

Printed in Malaysia

Lot #:
4 6 8 10 9 7 5

05/23

unionsquareandco.com

Interior design by Heather Kelly

THE BOY WHO THOUGHT OUTSIDE THE BOX

THE STORY OF VIDEO GAME INVENTOR RALPH BAER

BY MARCIE WESSELS

ILLUSTRATED BY BEATRIZ CASTRO

union square kids

NEW YORK

On the streets of Cologne, Germany,
a boy named Ralph Baer made his own fun.

He rolled hoops on the sidewalk.

He raced his scooter.

He played stick hockey
and biked with his
best friend, Herbert.

Ralph played freely until being outside became too dangerous for a Jewish kid like him.

Hitler, the leader of Germany, blamed the country's problems on Jewish people.

He ordered his Nazi soldiers to attack Jews and other groups he disliked.

Fear and hatred grew and grew.

Boys in Ralph's neighborhood became bullies.

They called Ralph names and tried to steal his bike.

Even former friends became enemies.

With no one to play with, Ralph spent more time indoors, tinkering with his construction set. He connected girders and gears, rods and brackets, pulleys and plates. The models in the manual were a cinch! Ideas for new inventions whirled and swirled in Ralph's brain. To build them, he needed more parts.

But money was scarce. Ralph would have to make do with what he had. How else might he use the pieces and parts around him? He loved to configure and reconfigure—to invent!

Ralph was a boy who thought outside the box.

While Ralph built with his construction set,
the Nazis built walls to keep Germans in and Jews out.

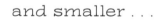

Ralph's world grew
smaller . . .

and smaller . . .

and smaller.

At fourteen, he was kicked out of school because he was Jewish.

But nothing could box Ralph into a corner.

He kept studying on his own. He learned English and helped his family obtain visas to immigrate to the United States.

In August 1938, Ralph and his family fled Germany.

As newly arrived immigrants in New York, Ralph and his father found jobs at a leather goods factory.

During the day, Ralph attached buttons to cosmetic cases.

To make extra money, he brought piecework home at night.

Ralph and his sister marked the leather by hand.

Their mother sewed the pieces together.

The whole family worked to rebuild their lives.

Punch. Sew. Punch. Sew.

Could Ralph make their work go faster?

He brainstormed a solution . . .
drew up a design . . .
and built a prototype.

PUNCH.
PUNCH.
PUNCH.
PUNCH.
PUNCH.

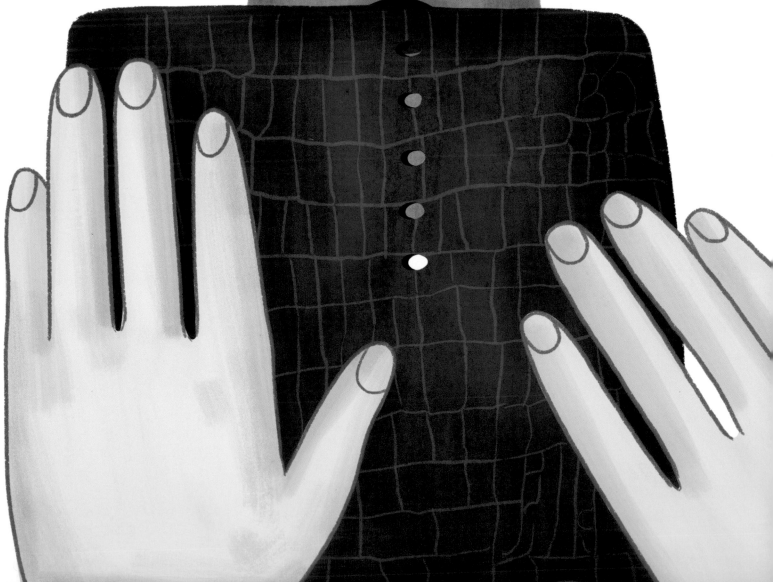

Ralph's first invention worked! Now the family could sew twice as many cases in the same amount of time.

Ralph's curiosity couldn't be contained. Radio was all the rage, and Ralph wondered how the boxes of talk and music worked.

The seventeen-year-old boy saved up his money and took a radio repair course. Soon, he was fixing radios for the entire neighborhood.

At the age of twenty-one, Ralph was drafted into the Army. At night, he and the other soldiers longed for news and entertainment. Ralph knew how to repair radios, but could he build one?

He rounded up spare parts and started tinkering.

His bunkmates shook their heads. They thought it would never work.

But sure enough, Ralph had the barracks swinging in no time!

After the war, a box of sound and moving pictures captured Ralph's imagination. He packed up his toolbox and took the train from New York to Chicago to study at the American Television Institute of Technology.

By the end of the first semester, Ralph could build a TV set from scratch.

You are cordially invited

OPEN HOUSE

Television soon replaced radio as most families' source of news and entertainment. With only three networks, viewers tuned in to a handful of programs.

Most people thought TV was magical. Critics called it the "idiot box" for the way it captivated an audience.

Ralph saw it as a box full of possibilities.

After graduation, Ralph worked in a lab designing television sets. He used special testing equipment to draw lines and patterns on the screen.

One day, he looked at the display and imagined a different use for the TV.

Perhaps a television could be used to play games! Wouldn't that be fun?

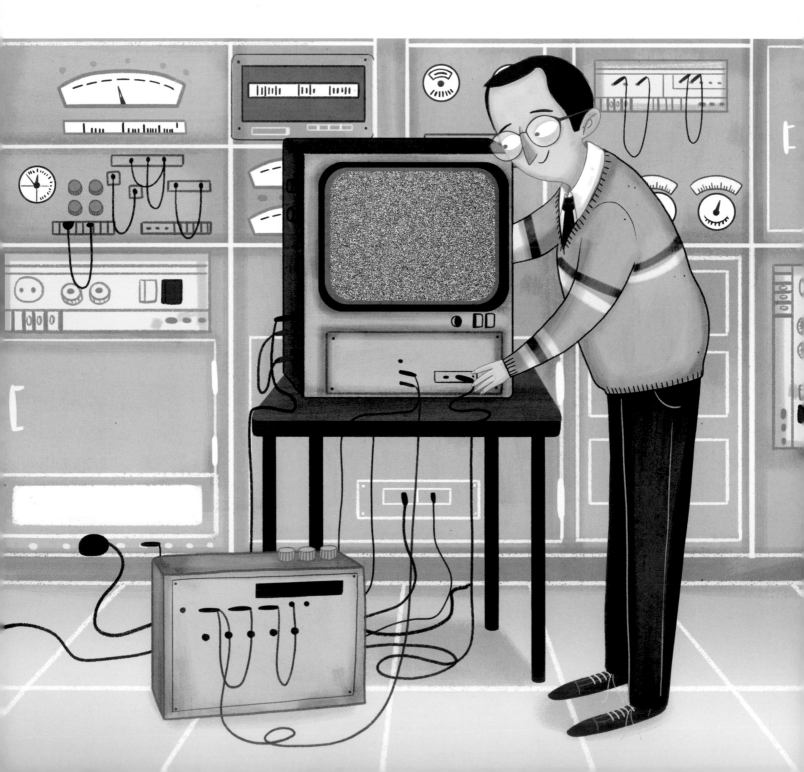

No one had ever played games on a TV before. In 1951, no one even dreamed of it.

Except Ralph.

He tried to convince his boss to build games directly into television consoles. The boss dismissed Ralph's idea.

Disappointed, Ralph boxed up his idea and shelved it away in a corner of his mind.

Over the next fifteen years, Ralph built electronic equipment for the U.S. military and for NASA.

He developed spy equipment to listen in on Russian radio transmissions.

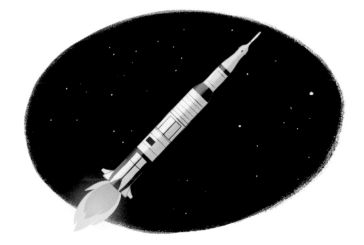

He made a display console to monitor the Saturn V rocket.

He embedded a radio transmitter in the handle of the video camera that astronaut Neil Armstrong took to the moon.

He learned to put electronics in smaller and smaller spaces.

One day in 1966, while waiting for his bus, Ralph unboxed his original gaming idea.

Instead of building games directly into a television set, he imagined using an external box to control the TV to play games.

Action games! Board games! Educational games! Sports!

Ralph drew up a design and got to work.

Ralph had a new boss who loved his out-of-the-box thinking. He gave Ralph the money and people power to develop his idea.

In a secret lab, Ralph and three other engineers built a box full of tubes, wires, and circuits. They adjusted switches and knobs to make a line on the screen. They created a ball that could bounce around.

Their work felt like play.
Everyone in the building wanted a turn!

Over the next year, Ralph and his team tweaked their project,
adding color, accessories, and sound.

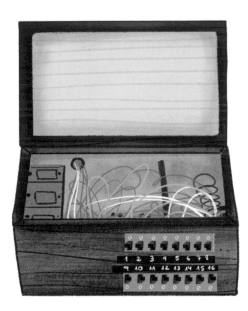

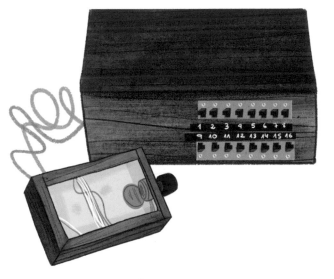

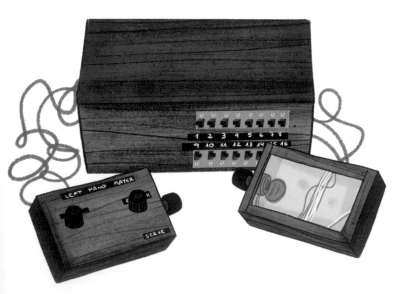

They built seven prototypes and wrapped the last one in sticky wood-grained paper. Ralph's home TV game system, the Brown Box, was born!

To get his console into people's homes, Ralph needed to make more. A *lot* more. To do this, he would need the support of a commercial electronics company.

Ralph showed his Brown Box to cable and TV companies everywhere, but no one thought playing games on a television set was a good idea.

Again and again, Ralph's idea was rejected.

Finally, one company was inspired by Ralph's enthusiasm and vision. Magnavox agreed to create a simpler box based on Ralph's design.

In 1972, the Magnavox Odyssey hit store shelves.

For the first time ever, people discovered a fun new way to use their TV!

After the Odyssey, Ralph invented other electronic toys and games.

He left the video game industry in 1975. But his work inspired other people to advance this form of home entertainment.

Radio technician

Television designer

Electronics engineer

Video game pioneer

Toy and game inventor

Ralph Baer forever changed the way we play.

AUTHOR'S NOTE

Over the last fifty years, video games have become an integral part of our culture. But before 1972, there was no way for the average person to play video games at home. The earliest video games were created in the 1950s by computer scientists and mathematicians at British and North American universities. The simple games and simulations developed as part of their research and could only be played on enormous mainframe computers in academic laboratories.

As students at these universities learned to program the computers, they designed other games—sport, puzzle, card, logic and board—but their creations remained trapped in the lab. Computers and their components were still too expensive for the average consumer.

Television sets, on the other hand, were prevalent because of lower-cost electronic components. By the mid-1960s, there were over forty million TV sets in the United States alone.

Ralph's game box idea sparked a technological revolution in the electronics industry. Today's home video game consoles such as Wii, PlayStation, and Xbox are descendants of Ralph's Brown Box.

Ralph's ability to reimagine, repurpose, and reconfigure an everyday object was an inherent part of his personality. He is best known for his contribution to the video game industry, earning the nickname "The Father of Videogames," but Ralph also invented several toys, including the ever-popular electronic game *Simon*.

Ralph was awarded the National Medal of Technology in 2006, and in 2010 he was inducted into the National Inventors Hall of Fame. His workbench and a prototype of the Brown Box can be found in the Smithsonian Museum in Washington, D.C.

ADDITIONAL READING

Carson, Mary Kay. *Who Invented Home Video Games? Ralph Baer.* Berkeley Heights, NJ: Enslow Elementary, 2012.

Dickmann, Nancy. *The Man Behind Video Games.* North Mankato, MN: Pebble, 2019.

Frederick, Shane. *Gamers Unite! The Video Game Revolution.* Mankato, MN: Compass Point Books, 2010.

Hansen, Dustin. *Game On! Video Game History from Pong and Pac-Man to Mario, Minecraft, and More.* New York, NY: Feiwel & Friends, 2016.

Hile, Kevin. *Video Games.* Detroit, MI: Lucent Books, 2010.

Kaplan, Arie. *The Epic Evolution of Video Games.* Minneapolis, MN: Lerner Publications, 2014.

Maltman, Thomas James. *The Electrifying, Action-Packed, Unusual History of Video Games.* Mankato, MN: Capstone Press, 2011.

Wyckoff, Edwin Brit. *The Guy Who Invented Home Video Games: Ralph Baer and His Awesome Invention.* Berkeley Heights, NJ: Enslow Elementary, 2011.